GREAT AMERICAN POETS

GREAT AMERICAN POETS

Walt
Whitman

Edited and with an introduction
by Geoffrey Moore

 Clarkson N. Potter, Inc./Publishers NEW YORK
DISTRIBUTED BY CROWN PUBLISHERS, INC.

Published in the United States by Clarkson N. Potter, Inc.,
225 Park Avenue South, New York, New York 10003
and represented in Canada by the Canadian MANDA Group.
Published in Great Britain by Aurum Press Limited,
33 Museum Street, London WC1A 1LD, England

CLARKSON N. POTTER, POTTER, THE GREAT POETS,
and colophon are trademarks of Clarkson N. Potter, Inc.

Picture research by Juliet Brightmore

Manufactured in Hong Kong

Library of Congress Cataloging-in-Publication Data

Whitman, Walt, 1819–1892.
   Walt Whitman.

   (Great American Poets)
   I. Moore, Geoffrey. 2. Series.
PS3204   1987b   811'.3   87–14478
ISBN 0–517–56707–5

   10 9 8 7 6 5 4 3 2 1

   First Edition

CONTENTS

INTRODUCTION

In 1855 Walt Whitman published his first book of poems, which he printed and designed himself. It was called *Leaves of Grass*, a slim green volume with gold tendrils of grass but no name on the cover, and a daguerrotype of the author as the frontispiece, hand on hip, hat at the slouch, indolent, free, a lover of life. That at least was the pose, and one which Whitman preserved all his life.

He sent a copy to Ralph Waldo Emerson, the most famous American writer of his day. It was, said Emerson in his reply, 'the most extraordinary piece of wit and wisdom that America has yet contributed'. Whitman was so overjoyed at receiving such encouragement that he printed Emerson's letter without permission in the next edition, much to Emerson's annoyance.

It was, in fact, a remarkable book to have been produced by a man in his early thirties, a book without precedent in the history of English poetry, free – indeed, to the early nineteenth-century eye, prosy – in its style, full of large sympathies and large gestures and, above all, loving, Christlike, in its attitude towards mankind.

Who was this extraordinary man? He had been born of an ordinary Long Island family in 1819, his father a carpenter and one-time farmer descended from an English family which had come over in the seventeenth century, his mother equally uneducated, of English and Welsh stock. When Walt was five his family moved to Brooklyn, where he was educated in public schools until he was twelve. It was in Brooklyn that he began his association with 'powerful uneducated persons' as well as with the well-known writers and politicians of his day. At the age of twenty-seven he became editor of the *Brooklyn Daily Eagle* in which he voiced the progressive opinions of his day: Transcendentalism, a buoyant nationalism, a burning desire for the improvement of society, opposition to slavery.

After the publication of *Leaves of Grass* it became abundantly clear how different Whitman was from his predecessors. He was the first great Original of the American scene, and he was so not only because of his native genius but also because he was the child of his age. He needed America as much as America needed him – to throw off the shackles of what Hawthorne sentimentally called 'our old Home' and develop a style, an idiom and, above all, a message which would embody the spirit of a great new nation.

The secret of his success lay in the nature of the poetic convention which he invented. He used not the 'I' which was himself but the 'I' which embodied mankind, a 'voyaging ego' through which he could express hopes and fears which might seem personal but which were common to all men in all nations. As he himself said, 'I have but one central figure, the general human personality typified in myself. But my book compels, absolutely necessitates, every reader to transpose himself or herself into the central position, and become the living fountain, actor, experiencer himself, or herself, of every page, every aspiration, every line.' And so it does – if the reader immerses himself (or herself) in what is still for some an 'unpoetic' style. Forget rhyme and give yourself up to a new rhythm; you will find a subtle, personal use of words working under the apparently flat series of statements.

Whitman was the great innovator of his time, the poet of and for the people, the writer who was the direct ancestor of William Carlos Williams and Allen Ginsberg. He opened up America to poetry as surely as the transcontinental railroad opened up the Pacific to the nation – even though it took a hundred years for the long drawn out battle to be completely won. One may look at the changes in Robert Lowell's style, and in John Berryman's, as in the 1950s they started to come to terms with what the Beat and the Black Mountain poets had started. They were only responding to the spirit of Pound and Williams, and they in their turn to the spirit of Whitman before them. He is the father of them all.

But not in his lifetime. In his lifetime he was often reviled – and he answered by showing the sweetness and goodness of his nature when working as a wound-dresser in the war between the States. Gore Vidal in *Lincoln* depicts him rather pathetically turning up in the forerunner of the Oval Office to seek political favour. Whitman did, in fact, become a government clerk in Washington until 1873 when he was stricken with paralysis. He then retired to his little house in Camden, New Jersey, where he spent the last nineteen years of his life being visited by the most forward-looking spirits of many nations. Gerard Manley Hopkins expressed great sympathy; William Michael Rossetti presented him to the English public; John Addington Symons wrote an appreciative biography. His work was translated into German, Danish and French, and was soon known all round the world. He studied the greatest; he thought the highest; there was nothing base in his nature.

GEOFFREY MOORE

There Was a Child Went Forth

There was a child went forth every day,
And the first object he look'd upon, that object he
    became,
And that object became part of him for the day or a
    certain part of the day,
Or for many years or stretching cycles of years.

The early lilacs became part of this child,
And grass and white and red morning-glories, and
    white and red clover, and the song of the
    phoebe-bird,
And the Third-month lambs and the sow's pink-
    faint litter, and the mare's foal and the cow's
    calf,
And the noisy brood of the barnyard or by the mire
    of the pond-side,
And the fish suspending themselves so curiously
    below there, and the beautiful curious liquid,
And the water-plants with their graceful flat heads,
    all became part of him.

The field-sprouts of Fourth-month and Fifth-
    month became part of him,
Winter-grain sprouts and those of the light-yellow
    corn, and the esculent roots of the garden,
And the apple-trees cover'd with blossoms and the
    fruit afterward, and wood-berries, and the
    commonest weeds by the road,
And the old drunkard staggering home from the out-
    house of the tavern whence he had lately risen,

And the schoolmistress that pass'd on her way to
   the school,
And the friendly boys that pass'd, and the
   quarrelsome boys,
And the tidy and fresh-cheek'd girls, and the
   barefoot negro boy and girl,
And all the changes of city and country wherever
   he went.

His own parents, he that had father'd him and she
   that had conceiv'd him in her womb and
   birth'd him,
They gave this child more of themselves than that,
They gave him afterward every day, they became
   part of him.

The mother at home quietly placing the dishes on
   the supper-table,
The mother with mild words, clean her cap and
   gown, a wholesome odor falling off her person
   and clothes as she walks by,
The father, strong, self-sufficient, manly, mean,
   anger'd, unjust,
The blow, the quick loud word, the tight bargain,
   the crafty lure,
The family usages, the language, the company, the
   furniture, the yearning and swelling heart,
Affection that will not be gainsay'd, the sense of
   what is real, the thought if after all it should
   prove unreal,

The doubts of day-time and the doubts of night-
time, the curious whether and how,
Whether that which appears so is so, or is it all
flashes and specks?
Men and women crowding fast in the streets, if
they are not flashes and specks what are they?
The streets themselves and the façades of houses,
and goods in the windows,
Vehicles, teams, the heavy-plank'd wharves, the
huge crossing at the ferries,
The village on the highland seen from afar at
sunset, the river between,
Shadows, aureola and mist, the light falling on roofs
and gables of white or brown two miles off,
The schooner near by sleepily dropping down the
tide, the little boat slack-tow'd astern,
The hurrying tumbling waves, quick-broken crests,
slapping,
The strata of color'd clouds, the long bar of
maroon-tint away solitary by itself, the spread
of purity it lies motionless in,
The horizon's edge, the flying sea-crow, the
fragrance of salt marsh and shore mud,
These became part of that child who went forth
every day, and who now goes, and will always
go forth every day.

Song of Myself

1

I celebrate myself, and sing myself,
And what I assume you shall assume,
For every atom belonging to me as good belongs to
    you.

I loafe and invite my soul,
I lean and loafe at my ease observing a spear of
    summer grass.

My tongue, every atom of my blood, form'd from
    this soil, this air,
Born here of parents born here from parents the
    same, and their parents the same,
I, now thirty-seven years old in perfect health begin,
Hoping to cease not till death.

Creeds and schools in abeyance,
Retiring back a while sufficed at what they are, but
    never forgotten,
I harbor for good or bad, I permit to speak at every
    hazard,
Nature without check with original energy.

2

Houses and rooms are full of perfumes, the shelves
    are crowded with perfumes,
I breathe the fragrance myself and know it and like it,
The distillation would intoxicate me also, but I
    shall not let it.

The atmosphere is not a perfume, it has no taste of
      the distillation, it is odorless,
It is for my mouth forever, I am in love with it,
I will go to the bank by the wood and become
      undisguised and naked,
I am mad for it to be in contact with me.

The smoke of my own breath,
Echoes, ripples, buzz'd whispers, love-root, silk-
      thread, crotch and vine,
My respiration and inspiration, the beating of my
      heart, the passing of blood and air through my
      lungs,
The sniff of green leaves and dry leaves, and of the
      shore and dark-color'd sea-rocks, and hay in
      the barn,
The sound of the belch'd words of my voice loos'd
      to the eddies of the wind,
A few light kisses, a few embraces, a reaching
      around of arms,
The play of shine and shade on the trees as the
      supple boughs wag,
The delight alone or in the rush of the streets, or
      along the fields and hill-sides,
The feeling of health, the full-noon trill, the song
      of me rising from bed and meeting the sun.

Have you reckon'd a thousand acres much? have
      you reckon'd the earth much?
Have you practis'd so long to learn to read?
Have you felt so proud to get at the meaning of poems?

Stop this day and night with me and you shall
        possess the origin of all poems,
You shall possess the good of the earth and sun,
        (there are millions of suns left,)
You shall no longer take things at second or third
        hand, nor look through the eyes of the dead,
        nor feed on the spectres in books,
You shall not look through my eyes either, nor take
        things from me,
You shall listen to all sides and filter them from
        your self.

3

I have heard what the talkers were talking, the talk
        of the beginning and the end,
But I do not talk of the beginning or the end.

There was never any more inception than there is now
Nor any more youth or age than there is now,
And will never be any more perfection than there
        is now,
Nor any more heaven or hell than there is now.

Urge and urge and urge,
Always the procreant urge of the world.
Out of the dimness opposite equals advance, always
        substance and increase, always sex,
Always a knit of identity, always distinction,
        always a breed of life.

To elaborate is no avail, learn'd and unlearn'd feel
        that it is so.

Sure as the most certain sure, plumb in the
    uprights, well entretied, braced in the beams,
Stout as a horse, affectionate, haughty, electrical,
I and this mystery here we stand.

Clear and sweet is my soul, and clear and sweet is
    all that is not my soul.

Lack one lacks both, and the unseen is proved by
    the seen,
Till that becomes unseen and receives proof in its turn.

Showing the best and dividing it from the worst age
    vexes age,
Knowing the perfect fitness and equanimity of
    things, while they discuss I am silent, and go
    bathe and admire myself.
Welcome is every organ and attribute of me, and of
    any man hearty and clean,
Not an inch nor a particle of an inch is vile, and
    none shall be less familiar than the rest.

I am satisfied—I see, dance, laugh, sing;
As the hugging and loving bed-fellow sleeps at my
    side through the night, and withdraws at the
    peep of the day with stealthy tread,
Leaving me baskets cover'd with white towels
    swelling the house with their plenty,
Shall I postpone my acceptation and realization
    and scream at my eyes,
That they turn from gazing after and down the road,
And forthwith cipher and show me to a cent,

Exactly the value of one and exactly the value of
    two, and which is ahead?

4

Trippers and askers surround me,
People I meet, the effect upon me of my early life or
    the ward and city I live in, or the nation,
The latest dates, discoveries, inventions, societies,
    authors old and new,
My dinner, dress, associates, looks, compliments,
    dues,
The real or fancied indifference of some man or
    woman I love,
The sickness of one of my folks or of myself, or
    ill-doing or loss or lack of money, or
    depressions or exaltations,
Battles, the horrors of fratricidal war, the fever of
    doubtful news, the fitful events;
These come to me days and nights and go from me
    again,
But they are not the Me myself.

Apart from the pulling and hauling stands what I am,
Stands amused, complacent, compassionating,
    idle, unitary,
Looks down, is erect, or bends an arm on an
    impalpable certain rest,
Looking with side-curved head curious what will
    come next,
Both in and out of the game and watching and
    wondering at it.

Backward I see in my own days where I sweated
    through fog with linguists and contenders,
I have no mockings or arguments, I witness and wait.

5

I believe in you my soul, the other I am must not
    abase itself to you,
And you must not be abased to the other.

Loafe with me on the grass, loose the stop from
    your throat,
Not words, not music or rhyme I want, not custom
    or lecture, not even the best,
Only the lull I like, the hum of your valvèd voice.

I mind how once we lay such a transparent summer
    morning,
How you settled your head athwart my hips and
    gently turn'd over upon me,
And parted the shirt from my bosom-bone, and
    plunged your tongue to my bare-stript heart,
And reach'd till you felt my beard, and reach'd till
    you held my feet.

Swiftly arose and spread around me the peace and know-
    ledge that pass all the argument of the earth,
And I know that the hand of God is the promise of
    my own,
And I know that the spirit of God is the brother of
    my own,
And that all the men ever born are also my brothers, an
    the women my sisters and lovers,

And that a kelson of the creation is love,
And limitless are leaves stiff or drooping in the
    fields,
And brown ants in the little wells beneath them,
And the mossy scabs of the worm fence, heap'd
    stones, elder, mullein and poke-weed.

6

A child said *What is the grass?* fetching it to me with
    full hands,
How could I answer the child? I do not know what
    it is any more than he.

I guess it must be the flag of my disposition, out of
    hopeful green stuff woven.

Or I guess it is the handkerchief of the Lord,
A scented gift and remembrancer designedly dropt,
Bearing the owner's name someway in the corners,
    that we may see and remark, and say *Whose?*

Or I guess the grass is itself a child, the produced
    babe of the vegetation.

Or I guess it is a uniform hieroglyphic,
And it means, Sprouting alike in broad zones and
    narrow zones,
Growing among black folks as among white,
Kanuck, Tuckahoe, Congressman, Cuff, I give
    them the same, I receive them the same.

And now it seems to me the beautiful uncut hair of
    graves.

Tenderly will I use you curling grass,
It may be you transpire from the breasts of young men,
It may be if I had known them I would have loved them,
It may be you are from old people, or from offspring
    taken soon out of their mothers' laps,
And here you are the mothers' laps.

This grass is very dark to be from the white heads of
    old mothers,
Darker than the colourless beards of old men,
Dark to come from under the faint red roofs of mouths.

O I perceive after all so many uttering tongues,
And I perceive they do not come from the roofs of
    mouths for nothing.

I wish I could translate the hints about the dead
    young men and women,
And the hints about old men and mothers, and the
    offspring taken soon out of their laps.

What do you think has become of the young and
    old men?
And what do you think has become of the women
    and children?

They are alive and well somewhere,
The smallest sprout shows there is really no death,
And if ever there was it led forward life, and does
    not wait at the end to arrest it,
And ceas'd the moment life appear'd.
All goes onward and outward, nothing collapses,
And to die is different from what any one supposed,
    and luckier.

Has any one supposed it lucky to be born?
I hasten to inform him or her it is just as lucky to
    die, and I know it.

I pass death with the dying and birth with the
    new-wash'd babe, and am not contain'd
    between my hat and boots,
And peruse manifold objects, no two alike and
    every one good,
The earth good and the stars good, and their
    adjuncts all good.

I am not an earth nor an adjunct of an earth,
I am the mate and companion of people, all just as
    immortal and fathomless as myself,
(They do not know how immortal, but I know.)

Every kind for itself and its own, for me mine male
    and female,
For me those that have been boys and that love women
For me the man that is proud and feels how it stings
    to be slighted,
For me the sweet-heart and the old maid, for me
    mothers and the mothers of mothers,
For me lips that have smiled, eyes that have shed tears,
For me children and the begetters of children.

Undrape! you are not guilty to me, nor stale nor
    discarded,
I see through the broadcloth and gingham whether
    or no,

And am around, tenacious, acquisitive, tireless,
    and cannot be shaken away.

8

The little one sleeps in its cradle,
I lift the gauze and look a long time, and silently
    brush away flies with my hand.

The youngster and the red-faced girl turn aside up
    the bushy hill,
I peeringly view them from the top.

The suicide sprawls on the bloody floor of the bedroom,
I witness the corpse with its dabbled hair, I note
    where the pistol has fallen.

The blab of the pave, tires of carts, sluff of
    boot-soles, talk of the promenaders,
The heavy omnibus, the driver with his
    interrogating thumb, the clank of the shod
    horses on the granite floor,
The snow-sleighs, clinking, shouted jokes, pelts of
    snow-balls,
The hurrahs for popular favorites, the fury of rous'd
    mobs,
The flap of the curtain'd litter, a sick man inside
    borne to the hospital,
The meeting of enemies, the sudden oath, the
    blows and fall,
The excited crowd, the policeman with his star
    quickly working his passage to the centre of
    the crowd,

The impassive stones that receive and return so
     many echoes,
What groans of over-fed or half-starv'd who fall
     sunstruck or in fits,
What exclamations of women taken suddenly who
     hurry home and give birth to babes,
What living and buried speech is always vibrating
     here, what howls restrain'd by decorum,
Arrests of criminals, slights, adulterous offers made,
     acceptances, rejections with convex lips,
I mind them or the show or resonance of them – I
     come and I depart.

9

The big doors of the country barn stand open and ready,
The dried grass of the harvest-time loads the
     slow-drawn wagon,
The clear light plays on the brown gray and green
     intertinged,
The armfuls are pack'd to the sagging mow.

I am there, I help, I came stretch'd atop of the load,
I felt its soft jolts, one leg reclined on the other,
I jump from the cross-beams and seize the clover
     and timothy,
And roll head over heels and tangle my hair full of
     wisps.

10

Alone far in the wilds and mountains I hunt,
Wandering amazed at my own lightness and glee,

In the late afternoon choosing a safe spot to pass
    the night,
Kindling a fire and broiling the fresh-kill'd game,
Falling asleep on the gather'd leaves with my dog
    and gun by my side.

The Yankee clipper is under her sky-sails, she cuts
    the sparkle and scud,
My eyes settle the land, I bend at her prow or shout
    joyously from the deck.

The boatmen and clam-diggers arose early and
    stopt for me,
I tuck'd my trowser-ends in my boots and went and
    had a good time;
You should have been with us that day round the
    chowder-kettle.

I saw the marriage of the trapper in the open air in
    the far west, the bride was a red girl,
Her father and his friends sat near cross-legged and
    dumbly smoking, they had moccasins to their
    feet and large thick blankets hanging from
    their shoulders,
On a bank lounged the trapper, he was drest mostly in
    skins, his luxuriant beard and curls protected his
    neck, he held his bride by the hand,
She had long eyelashes, her head was bare, her
    coarse straight locks descended upon her
    voluptuous limbs and reach'd to her feet.

The runaway slave came to my house and stopt
    outside,

I heard his motions crackling the twigs of the
      woodpile,
Through the swung half-door of the kitchen I saw
      him limpsy and weak,
And went where he sat on a log and led him in and
      assured him,
And brought water and fill'd a tub for his sweated
      body and bruis'd feet,
And gave him a room that enter'd from my own,
      and gave him some coarse clean clothes,
And remember perfectly well his revolving eyes
      and his awkwardness,
And remember putting plasters on the galls of his
      neck and ankles;
He staid with me a week before he was recuperated
      and pass'd north,
I had him sit next me at table, my fire-lock lean'd
      in the corner.

11

Twenty-eight young men bathe by the shore,
Twenty-eight young men and all so friendly;
Twenty-eight years of womanly life and all so
      lonesome.

She owns the fine house by the rise of the bank,
She hides handsome and richly drest aft the blinds
      of the window.

Which of the young men does she like the best?
Ah the homeliest of them is beautiful to her.

Where are you off to, lady? for I see you,
You splash in the water there, yet stay stock still in
    your room.

Dancing and laughing along the beach came the
    twenty-ninth bather,
The rest did not see her, but she saw them and
    loved them.

The beards of the young men glisten'd with wet, it
    ran from their long hair,
Little streams pass'd all over their bodies.

An unseen hand also pass'd over their bodies,
It descended tremblingly from their temples and ribs

The young men float on their backs, their white
    bellies bulge to the sun, they do not ask who
    seizes fast to them,
They do not know who puffs and declines with
    pendant and bending arch,
They do not think whom they souse with spray.

12

The butcher-boy puts off his killing-clothes, or
    sharpens his knife at the stall in the market,
I loiter enjoying his repartee and his shuffle and
    break-down.

Blacksmiths with grimed and hairy chests environ
    the anvil,
Each has his main-sledge, they are all out, there is a
    great heat in the fire.

From the cider-strew'd threshold I follow their
        movements,
The lithe sheer of their waists plays even with their
        massive arms,
Overhand the hammers swing, overhand so slow,
        overhand so sure,
They do not hasten, each man hits in his place.

13

The negro holds firmly the reins of his four horses,
        the block swags underneath on its tied-over
        chain,
The negro that drives the long dray of the
        stone-yard, steady and tall he stands pois'd on
        one leg on the string-piece,
His blue shirt exposes his ample neck and breast
        and loosens over his hip-band,
His glance is calm and commanding, he tosses the
        slouch of his hat away from his forehead,
The sun falls on his crispy hair and mustache, falls
        on the black of his polish'd and perfect limbs.

I behold the picturesque giant and love him, and I
        do not stop there,
I go with the team also.

In me the caresser of life wherever moving,
        backward as well as forward sluing,
To niches aside and junior bending, not a person or
        object missing,
Absorbing all to myself and for this song.

Oxen that rattle the yoke and chain or halt in the
    leafy shade, what is that you express in your
    eyes?
It seems to me more than all the print I have read
    in my life.

My tread scares the wood-drake and wood-duck on
    my distant and day-long ramble,
They rise together, they slowly circle around.

I believe in those wing'd purposes,
And acknowledge red, yellow, white, playing
    within me,
And consider green and violet and the tufted
    crown intentional,
And do not call the tortoise unworthy because she
    is not something else,
And the jay in the woods never studied the gamut,
    yet trills pretty well to me,
And the look of the bay mare shames silliness out
    of me.

14

The wild gander leads his flock through the cool
    night,
Ya-honk he says, and sounds it down to me like an
    invitation,
The pert may suppose it meaningless, but I
    listening close,
Find its purpose and place up there toward the
    wintry sky.

The sharp-hoof'd moose of the north, the cat on
      the house-sill, the chickadee, the prairie-dog,
The litter of the grunting sow as they tug at her
      teats,
The brood of the turkey-hen and she with her
      half-spread wings,
I see in them and myself the same old law.

The press of my foot to the earth springs a hundred
      affections,
They scorn the best I can do to relate them.

I am enamour'd of growing out-doors,
Of men that live among cattle or taste of the ocean
      or woods,
Of the builders and steerers of ships and the
      wielders of axes and mauls, and the drivers of
      horses,
I can eat and sleep with them week in and week
      out.

What is commonest, cheapest, nearest, easiest, is
      Me,
Me going in for my chances, spending for vast
      returns,
Adorning myself to bestow myself on the first that
      will take me,
Not asking the sky to come down to my good will,
Scattering it freely forever.

I Saw in Louisiana a Live-Oak Growing

I saw in Louisiana a live-oak growing,
All alone stood it and the moss hung down from
the branches,
Without any companion it grew there uttering
joyous leaves of dark green,
And its look, rude, unbending, lusty, made me
think of myself,
But I wonder'd how it could utter joyous leaves
standing alone there without its friend near,
for I knew I could not,
And I broke off a twig with a certain number of
leaves upon it, and twined around it a little
moss,
And brought it away, and I have placed it in sight,
in my room,
It is not needed to remind me as of my own dear
friends,
(For I believe lately I think of little else than of
them,)
Yet it remains to me a curious token, it makes me
think of manly love;
For all that, and though the live-oak glistens there
in Louisiana solitary in a wide flat space,
Uttering joyous leaves all its life without a friend a
lover near,
I know very well I could not.

I Sit and Look Out

I sit and look out upon all the sorrows of the world,
and upon all oppression and shame,
I hear secret convulsive sobs from young men at
anguish with themselves, remorseful after
deeds done,
I see in low life the mother misused by her
children, dying, neglected, gaunt, desperate,
I see the wife misused by her husband, I see the
treacherous seducer of young women,
I mark the ranklings of jealousy and unrequited
love attempted to be hid, I see these sights on
the earth,
I see the workings of battle, pestilence, tyranny, I
see martyrs and prisoners,
I observe a famine at sea, I observe the sailors
casting lots who shall be kill'd to preserve the
lives of the rest,
I observe the slights and degradations cast by
arrogant persons upon laborers, the poor, and
upon negroes, and the like;
All these – all the meanness and agony without end
I sitting look out upon,
See, hear, and am silent.

Once I Pass'd Through
a Populous City

Once I pass'd through a populous city imprinting
    my brain for future use with its shows,
    architecture, customs, traditions,
Yet now of all that city I remember only a woman I
    casually met there who detain'd me for love of
    me,
Day by day and night by night we were together –
    all else has long been forgotten by me,
I remember I say only that woman who passionately
    clung to me,
Again we wander, we love, we separate again,
Again she holds me by the hand, I must not go,
I see her close beside me with silent lips sad and
    tremulous.

When Lilacs Last in the Dooryard Bloom'd

1

When lilacs last in the dooryard bloom'd,
And the great star early droop'd in the western sky
    in the night,
I mourn'd, and yet shall mourn with ever-returning
    spring.

Ever-returning spring, trinity sure to me you bring,
Lilac blooming perennial and drooping star in the
    west,
And thought of him I love.

2

O powerful western fallen star!
O shades of night – O moody, tearful night!
O great star disappear'd – O the black murk that
    hides the star!
O cruel hands that hold me powerless – O helpless
    soul of me!
O harsh surrounding cloud that will not free my soul.

3

In the dooryard fronting an old farm-house near the
    white-wash'd palings,
Stands the lilac-bush tall-growing with heart-shaped
    leaves of rich green,

With many a pointed blossom rising delicate, with
     the perfume strong I love,
With every leaf a miracle – and from this bush in
     the dooryard,
With delicate-color'd blossoms and heart-shaped
     leaves of rich green,
A sprig with its flower I break.

4

In the swamp in secluded recesses,
A shy and hidden bird is warbling a song.

Solitary the thrush,
The hermit withdrawn to himself, avoiding the
     settlements,
Sings by himself a song.

Song of the bleeding throat,
Death's outlet song of life, (for well dear brother I
     know, if thou wast not granted to sing thou
     would'st surely die.)

5

Over the breast of the spring, the land, amid cities,
Amid lanes and through old woods, where lately
     the violets peep'd from the ground, spotting
     the gray debris,
Amid the grass in the fields each side of the lanes,
     passing the endless grass,

Passing the yellow-spear'd wheat, every grain from
    its shroud in the dark-brown fields uprisen,
Passing the apple-tree blows of white and pink in
    the orchards,
Carrying a corpse to where it shall rest in the grave,
Night and day journeys a coffin.

6

Coffin that passes through lanes and streets,
Through day and night with the great cloud
    darkening the land,
With the pomp of the inloop'd flags with the cities
    draped in black,
With the show of the States themselves as of
    crape-veil'd women standing,
With processions long and winding and the
    flambeaus of the night,
With the countless torches lit, with the silent sea
    of faces and the unbared heads,
With the waiting depot, the arriving coffin, and
    the sombre faces,
With dirges through the night, with the thousand
    voices rising strong and solemn,
With all the mournful voices of the dirges pour'd
    around the coffin,
The dim-lit churches and the shuddering organs –
    where amid these you journey,
With the tolling tolling bells' perpetual clang,

Here, coffin that slowly passes,
I give you my sprig of lilac.

7

(Nor for you, for one alone,
Blossoms and branches green to coffins all I bring,
For fresh as the morning, thus would I chant a song
     for you O sane and sacred death.
All over bouquets of roses,
O death, I cover you over with roses and early lilies,
But mostly and now the lilac that blooms the first,
Copious I break, I break the sprigs from the bushes,
With loaded arms I come, pouring for you,
For you and the coffins all of you O death.)

8

O western orb sailing the heaven,
Now I know what you must have meant as a month
     since I walk'd,
As I walk'd in silence the transparent shadowy night,
As I saw you had something to tell as you bent to
     me night after night,
As you drooped from the sky low down as if to my
     side, (while the other stars all look'd on,)
As we wander'd together the solemn night, (for some-
     thing I know not what kept me from sleep,)

As the night advanced, and I saw on the rim of the
    west how full you were of woe,
As I stood on the rising ground in the breeze in the
    cool transparent night,
As I watch'd where you pass'd and was lost in the
    netherward black of the night,
As my soul in its trouble dissatisfied sank, as where
    you sad orb,
Concluded, dropt in the night, and was gone.

9

Sing on there in the swamp,
O singer bashful and tender, I hear your notes, I
    hear your call,
I hear, I come presently, I understand you,
But a moment I linger, for the lustrous star has
    detain'd me,
The star my departing comrade holds and detains me.

10

O how shall I warble myself for the dead one there I
    loved?
And how shall I deck my song for the large sweet
    soul that has gone?
And what shall my perfume be for the grave of him
    I love?

Sea-winds blown from east and west,

Blown from the Eastern sea and blown from the
    Western sea, till there on the prairies
    meeting,
These and with these and the breath of my chant,
I'll perfume the grave of him I love.

11

O what shall I hang on the chamber walls?
And what shall the pictures be that I hang on the
    walls,
To adorn the burial-house of him I love?

Pictures of growing spring and farms and homes,
With the Fourth-month eve at sundown, and the
    gray smoke lucid and bright,
With floods of the yellow gold of the gorgeous,
    indolent, sinking sun, burning, expanding the
    air,
With the fresh sweet herbage under foot, and the
    pale green leaves of the trees prolific,
In the distance the flowing glaze, the breast of the
    river, with a wind-dapple here and there,
With ranging hills on the banks, with many a line
    against the sky, and shadows,
And the city at hand with dwellings so dense, and
    stacks of chimneys,
And all the scenes of life and the workshops, and
    the workmen homeward returning.

Lo, body and soul – this land,
My own Manhattan with spires, and the sparkling
     and hurrying tides, and the ships,
The varied and ample land, the South and the
     North in the light, Ohio's shores and flashing
     Missouri,
And ever the far-spreading prairies cover'd with
     grass and corn.

Lo, the most excellent sun so calm and haughty,
The violet and purple morn with just-felt breezes,
The gentle soft-born measureless light,
The miracle spreading bathing all, the fulfill'd
     noon,
The coming eve delicious, the welcome night and
     the stars,
Over my cities shining all, enveloping man and land.

13

Sing on, sing on you gray-brown bird,
Sing from the swamps, the recesses, pour your
     chant from the bushes,
Limitless out of the dusk, out of the cedars and pines.

Sing on dearest brother, warble your reedy song,
Loud human song, with voice of uttermost woe.

O liquid and free and tender!
O wild and loose to my soul – O wondrous singer!

You only I hear – yet the star holds me, (but will
      soon depart,)
Yet the lilac with mastering odor holds me.

14

Now while I sat in the day and look'd forth,
In the close of the day with its light and the fields
      of spring, and the farmers preparing their
      crops,
In the large unconscious scenery of my land with its
      lakes and forests,
In the heavenly aerial beauty, (after the perturb'd
      winds and the storms,)
Under the arching heavens of the afternoon swift
      passing, and the voices of children and women,
The many-moving sea-tides, and I saw the ships
      how they sail'd,
And the summer approaching with richness, and
      the fields all busy with labor,
And the infinite separate houses, how they all went
      on, each with its meals and minutia of daily
      usages,
And the streets how their throbbings throbb'd, and
      the cities pent – lo, then and there,
Falling upon them all and among them all,
      enveloping me with the rest,
Appear'd the cloud, appear'd the long black trail,
And I knew death, its thought, and the sacred
      knowledge of death.

Then with the knowledge of death as walking one
    side of me,
And the thought of death close-walking the other
    side of me,
And I in the middle as with companions, and as
    holding the hands of companions,
I fled forth to the hiding receiving night that talks not,
Down to the shores of the water, the path by the
    swamp in the dimness,
To the solemn shadowy cedars and ghostly pines so
    still.

And the singer so shy to the rest receiv'd me,
The gray-brown bird I know receiv'd us comrades
    three,
And he sang the carol of death, and a verse for him
    I love.

From deep secluded recesses,
From the fragrant cedars and the ghostly pines so still,
Came the carol of the bird.

And the charm of the carol rapt me,
As I held as if by their hands my comrades in the
    night,
And the voice of my spirit tallied the song of the bird.

Come lovely and soothing death,
Undulate round the world, serenely arriving, arriving,
In the day, in the night, to all, to each,
Sooner or later delicate death.

Prais'd be the fathomless universe,
For life and joy, and for objects and knowledge curious,
And for love, sweet love – but praise! praise! praise!
For the sure-enwinding arms of cool-enfolding death.

Dark mother always gliding near with soft feet,
Have none chanted for thee a chant of fullest welcome?
Then I chant it for thee, I glorify thee above all,
I bring thee a song that when thou must indeed come,
        come unfalteringly.

Approach strong deliveress,
When it is so, when thou hast taken them I joyously
        sing the dead,
Lost in the loving floating ocean of thee,
Laved in the flood of thy bliss O death.

From me to thee glad serenades,
Dances for thee I propose saluting thee, adornments
        and feastings for thee,
And the sights of the open landscape and the high-spread
        sky are fitting,
And life and the fields, and the huge and thoughtful
        night.

The night in silence under many a star,
The ocean shore and the husky whispering wave whose
        voice I know,
And the soul turning to thee O vast and well-veil'd
        death,
And the body gratefully nestling close to thee.

Over the tree-tops I float thee a song,
Over the rising and sinking waves, over the myriad
    fields and the prairies wide,
Over the dense-pack'd cities all and the teeming
    wharves and ways,
I float this carol with joy, with joy to thee O death.

15

To the tally of my soul,
Loud and strong kept up the gray-brown bird,
With pure deliberate notes spreading filling the
    night.

Loud in the pines and cedars dim,
Clear in the freshness moist and the swamp-
    perfume,
And I with my comrades there in the night.

While my sight that was bound in my eyes
    unclosed,
As to long panoramas of visions.

And I saw askant the armies,
I saw as in noiseless dreams hundreds of battle-
    flags,
Borne through the smoke of the battles and pierc'd
    with missiles I saw them,
And carried hither and yon through the smoke,
    and torn and bloody,
And at last but a few shreds left on the staffs, (and
    all in silence,)
And the staffs all splinter'd and broken.

I saw battle-corpses, myriads of them,
And the white skeletons of young men, I saw them,
I saw the debris and debris of all the slain soldiers of
 the war,
But I saw they were not as was thought,
They themselves were fully at rest, they suffer'd not,
The living remain'd and suffer'd, the mother
 suffer'd,
And the wife and the child and the musing
 comrade suffer'd,
And the armies that remain'd suffer'd.

16

Passing the visions, passing the night,
Passing, unloosing the hold of my comrades' hands,
Passing the song of the hermit bird and the tallying
 song of my soul,
Victorious song, death's outlet song, yet varying
 ever-altering song,
As low and wailing, yet clear the notes, rising and
 falling, flooding the night,
Sadly sinking and fainting, as warning and
 warning, and yet again bursting with joy,
Covering the earth and filling the spread of the
 heaven,
As that powerful psalm in the night I heard from
 recesses,
Passing, I leave thee lilac with heart-shaped leaves,
I leave thee there in the door-yard, blooming,
 returning with spring.

I cease from my song for thee,
From my gaze on thee in the west, fronting the
      west, communing with thee,
O comrade lustrous with silver face in the night.

Yet each to keep and all, retrievements out of the
      night,
The song, the wondrous chant of the gray-brown
      bird,
And the tallying chant, the echo arous'd in my
      soul,
With the lustrous and drooping star with the
      countenance full of woe,
With the holders holding my hand nearing the call
      of the bird,
Comrades mine and I in the midst, and their
      memory ever to keep, for the dead I loved so
      well,
For the sweetest, wisest soul of all my days and
      lands – and this for his dear sake,
Lilac and star and bird twined with the chant of my
      soul,
There in the fragrant pines and the cedars dusk and
      dim.

NOTES ON THE PICTURES

p.6   *Pat Lyon at the Forge*, 1829, by John Neagle (1799–1865). Reproduced by courtesy of the Pennsylvania Academy of the Fine Arts. Gift of the Pat Lyon family.

p.15   *On a Lee Shore*, c. 1900, by Winslow Homer (1836–1910). Reproduced by courtesy of the Museum of Art, Rhode Island School of Design, Jesse Metcalf Fund.

p.18   *In Nature's Wonderland*, 1835, by Thomas Doughty (1793–1856). Reproduced by courtesy of the Detroit Institute of Arts, Gibbs–Williams Fund.

p.23   *Dancing on the Barn Floor*, 1831, by William Sidney Mount (1807–68). Reproduced by courtesy of the Suffolk Museum and Carriage House, Stony Brook, New York. Gift of Mr and Mrs Ward Melville, 1955. Photo: Bridgeman Art Library, London.

p.27   *Madonna of the Moors (Der Säugling)*, 1892, by Fritz Mackensen (1866–1953). Reproduced by courtesy of the Kunsthalle, Bremen, W. Germany.

p.30   *The Verdict of the People* (detail), 1854–55, by George Caleb Bingham (1811–79). Reproduced by courtesy of the Art Collection of the Boatmen's National Bank of St Louis, Missouri.

p.35   *The Swimming Hole*, 1883, by Thomas Eakins (1844–1916). Reproduced by courtesy of the Fort Worth Art Museum, Texas.

p.39   *Farmers Nooning*, 1836, by William Sidney Mount (1807–68). Reproduced by courtesy of the Suffolk Museum and Carriage House, Stony Brook, New York. Photo: Bridgeman Art Library, London.

p.43   *Portrait of Maud Cook*, 1895, by Thomas Eakins (1844–1916). Reproduced by courtesy of the Yale University Art Gallery, Connecticut. Bequeath of Stephen Carlton Clarke, B.A. 1903.

p.51   *In the Woods*, 1855, by Asher Brown Durand (1796–1886). Reproduced by courtesy of The Metropolitan Museum of Art, New York. Gift in memory of Jonathan Sturges by his children, 1895.

p.55   *The Timber Wagon*, by Atkinson Grimshaw (1836–93). Christopher Wood Gallery, London. Photo: Bridgeman Art Library, London.

p.58 *Twilight in the Wilderness*, 1860, by Frederic Edwin Church (1826–1900). Reproduced by courtesy of the Cleveland Museum of Art. Purchase, Mr and Mrs William H. Martlett Fund. Photo: Fabbri/Bridgeman Art Library, London.